T0374036

Chemistry Rhymes

A TOUR OF THE PERIODIC TABLE IN VERSE AND SONG

ALICE BAXTER

Illustrated by Ken Fredette

Chemistry Rhymes
A tour of the periodic table in verse and song

iUniverse books may be ordered through booksellers or by contacting:

iUniverse
1663 Liberty Drive
Bloomington, IN 47403
www.iuniverse.com
1-800-Authors (1-800-288-4677)

ISBN: 978-1-5320-9636-5 (sc)
ISBN: 978-1-5320-9637-2 (e)

Library of Congress Control Number: 2020903907

Print information available on the last page.

iUniverse rev. date: 03/06/2020

Hydrogen: Little Miss Muffet

Little miss hydrogen
Sat on an ottoman
Crying and sighing all day.
Along came a neutron
Who said "How do you do, hon,
And why are you so sad today?"

"Alas," she replied,
"I've nothing inside
But one lonely proton, that's all.
With nary a neutron,
To balance my proton,
Among elements I'm the oddball."

Neutron said, "Don't be glum
We'll make deuterium,
With a new mass of two and not one."
So they joined without fuss
Into one nucleus,
And made an isotope fit for the sun.

Helium: Mary Had a Little Lamb

Mary had some helium.
It had no taste or smell.
It would not burn, it was inert,
As far as she could tell.

She put some in a little glass,
But soon it disappeared.
And Mary said, "I think this gas
Is lighter than the air."

Then Mary got a big balloon.
She wanted it to fly.
She filled it with the helium
And launched it to the sky.

Lithium: Three Blind Mice

Three protons,
Three protons.
See how they run
To make lithium.
A shiny metal that cuts with a knife;
It was eagerly chased by the farmer's wife,
To make batteries stronger, with extra long life.
A good outcome
For lithium.

Boron and Beryllium: Tweedledum and Tweedledee

Boron and Beryllium
Resolved to have a battle,
For Boron said Beryllium
Was just a useless metal.

"But I," said Boron, "can make soap,
And when the need arises,
The boric acid that I form
Both cleans and sanitizes."

"Oh Boron," said Beryllium,
"At least I know I'm able
To find my proper place upon
The periodic table.

Remember that the table sorts
The elements quite neatly.
Metals left, non-metals right,
The rule applies completely.

But Boron, as a metalloid,
Where will you cast your lot?
Unlike me, you don't know if
You're metal or you're not."

Carbon: There Was an Old Woman Who Lived in a Shoe

There was an old carbon who lived in a shoe.
She made so many compounds, she didn't know what to do.
When she found other carbons, she couldn't refrain
From covalently bonding with them in a chain.

And bonding with carbons wasn't all she could do,
She grabbed hydrogen, oxygen and nitrogen too.
Long chain or short chain, sometimes in a ring,
These compounds of carbon could do anything.

There are sugars and starches, the fuels that we eat.
Hydrocarbons like methane will generate heat.
The aromas we smell and the flavors we taste,
Even paper and plastic are all carbon based.

Carbon is found in each part of a cell:
DNA, RNA, and enzymes as well.
Nine million compounds showed carbon her worth.
Without her there could be no life on this earth.

Nitrogen: Pussy cat, Pussy cat, Where have you been?

Nitrogen, nitrogen,
Where have you been?
"Traveling in circles
That make my head spin."

Nitrogen, nitrogen,
Where do you go?
"Air to soil, soil to air,
Back and forth, to and fro."

"Fixed in plants, free in air,
I never can stop.
Cause my nitrogen cycle
Is what grows all your crops."

Oxygen: Jack and Jill

Oxygen went down the glen
To fetch a drink of water.
The well was dry, which made him cry,
Cause the day was getting hotter.

Around the bend came hydrogen,
And said, "Don't be distraught, sir.
We'll bond just so, to make H_2O,
And there'll be lots of water."

Fluorine: Wee Willie Winkie

Wee Little Fluorine, runs through the town,
Looking for electrons, upstairs and down.
Electronegativity's as high as it can get,
She just needs one electron to have a full octet.

Searching all over, for atoms to attract,
A hyperactive halogen, she just wants to react.
If you are a metal, better run and hide.
Or she will ionize you, and make you a fluoride.

Neon: Simple Simon

Simple Simon found some neon
Floating in the air.
Said Simple Simon to the neon,
"Let's go to the fair."

Said the neon to Simple Simon,
"Why should I go with you?"
Said Simple Simon to the neon,
"It's the noble thing to do."

Said Simple Simon to the neon,
"We'll put on quite a show.
I'll plug you in, and cheers we'll win,
When people see you glow."

Sodium: Curly Locks, Curly Locks

Sodium, sodium,
Wilt thou be mine?
I'll find you some chlorine
And let you combine.

But if I then eat you,
It isn't my fault.
My food all tastes better
When I add some salt.

Magnesium: Diddle Diddle Dumpling, My Son John

Diddle Diddle dumpling, my son John
Found a piece of magnesium.
Shiny and bright to gaze upon;
Softer and much lighter than aluminum.

Diddle Diddle dumpling, John was dumb.
Tried to burn the magnesium.
Flared so bright that he burned his thumb.
Silly John just said "now that was fun."

Aluminum: Candle-Saving

To makes your cans last on and on,
Forever and a day-O.
Just make them from aluminum:
They'll never rust away-O.

Silicon: Down in the Valley

Down in the valley,
Where tech giants stand,
Silicon's flowing,
From everyday sand.

Semiconducting
Electricity,
Silcon's working
In every p.c.

A billion transistors
On one microchip,
Make smart phones responsive
To your fingertip.

Remember this lesson
Each time you log on.
You'd have no computer
Without silicon.

Phosphorus: Little Polly Flinders

Little Polly Flinders
Sat among the cinders,
With burns upon her pretty little toes.
She did something preposterous
And played with some white phosphorus,
Which caught on fire and burned up all her clothes.

Sulfur: I've Been Working on the Railroad

I've been excavating sulfur
All the live long day,
Manufacturing some compounds,
Just to pass the time away.

Fertilizers and explosives,
Acid for your batteries and more,
Don't you know they all are made from
H_2SO_4?

What's that awful smell? What's that awful smell?
Rotten eggs is what I guess, I guess.
What's that awful smell? What's that awful smell?
No, I think it's H_2S.

Chlorine: Take Me Out to the Ballgame

Take me out to go swimming,
Take me out to a pool.
Find me a pool where the water is clean.
I don't care if it smells like chlorine.

Cause chlorine's a great disinfectant,
But the gas is worse than benzene.
Cause with one, two, three gulps you're out,
If you breathe chlorine.

Argon: Lazy Mary

Lazy argon, will you react?
Will you react? Will you react?
Lazy argon, will you react
With any other atom?

No, said Argon, I won't react,
I won't react, I won't react.
Noble gases do not react.
My outer shell is quite full.

Potassium: Did You Ever See a Lassie?

Did you know you need potassium, potassium, potassium?
It's potassium that lets you move this way and that.
It travels through blood veins,
And crosses cell membranes,
So your cells can send out messages this way and that.

Did you know you need potassium, potassium, potassium?
Did you know you need potassium to make your heart beat?
Potassium ions
Charge muscles and neurons.
So be sure you get potassium in foods that you eat.

Calcium: Dem Bones

Dem bones, dem bones need calcium,
Dem bones, dem bones need calcium,
Dem bones, dem bones need calcium,
Make sure to drink your milk.

Now calcium's related to strontium,
And strontium's related to barium,
And barium's related to radium,
But if you ate those elements you'd be dumb,
They're no good for dem bones.

Dem bones, dem bones need calcium,
Dem bones, dem bones need calcium,
Dem bones, dem bones need calcium,
Make sure to drink your milk.

Scandium: Over in the Meadow

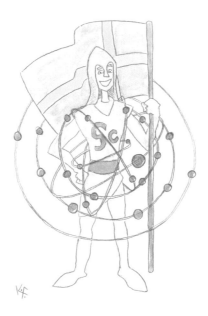

Over in the d block, you will find Scandium,
Discovered up in Sweden, underneath the midnight sun.
A shiny white metal,
Kind of like aluminum.
With electrons configured
4s2; 3d1

Titanium: Daisy, Daisy (Bicycle Built for Two)

Daisy, Daisy, give me your answer do.
I'm half crazy to try my new bike with you.
It's made from the perfect metal,
So easy for you to pedal.
You can't go wrong,
It's light and strong:
A titanium bike for two.

Michael, Michael, let me give you a tip.
Don't go biking where someone is apt to slip.
The bike's so light and shiny,
The pavement flew right by me.
Well thanks a lot,
'Cause now I've got,
Titanium in my hip.

Vanadium: Down by the Riverside

I'm gonna make my new sword and shield,
With steel and vanadium,
A drop of vanadium,
That's steel with vanadium.
For the strongest sword I can wield,
I need vanadium.
I'm gonna make some vanadium steel.

Chromium: Sing a Song of Sixpence

Sing a song of chromium.
It's found in chromite ore.
Four and twenty protons,
Packed in its core.

When electroplated,
It gives your stuff some bling.
It's just the perfect element
To set before a king.

The chauffeur shined the chrome upon
The royal limo wheels.
The cook used chromium to add
Some stainless to her steel.

The king was counting emeralds,
A gift to give his queen.
He did not know 'twas chromium
That made those jewels green.

Manganese: One Potato, Two Potato

One electron, two electron,
Three electron, four.
Managese can take electrons,
Five or six or more.

If you need an oxidizer,
Manganese is great.
Manganese dioxide works,
Or try permanganate.

Iron: London Bridge

KF.

London Bridge will not fall down,
Not fall down, not fall down,
Because the steel that holds it up
Is made with iron.

The earth has a magnetic field,
Magnetic field, magnetic field.
Because the core is molten hot,
And made from iron.

My blood carries oxygen,
Oxygen, oxygen.
Cause hemoglobin in my cells
Is made with iron.

Iron: London Bridge

Cobalt: Roses are Red

Roses are red,
Violets are blue.
If you contained cobalt,
You'd be blue too.

Nickel: Peter Piper

Peter Piper packed a stack of 50 nickels.
Just five grams weighed each nickel coin that Peter Piper packed.
If just a quarter of each coin is made from nickel metal,
What mass of nickel's in the stack that Peter Piper packed?

Copper: I'm a Little Teapot

I'm a copper teapot, short and stout.
I'm a great conductor, there is no doubt.
I boil water faster, hear me shout:
If your pot's aluminum, throw it out.

Zinc: The Itsy Bitsy Spider

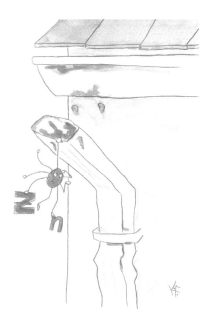

The itsy bitsy spider climbed up the water spout.
Down came the spout, 'cause it was rusted out.
Rats said the spider, I can't get a drink,
Because you did not galvanize the iron pipe with zinc.

Gallium: Oh Dear What Can the matter be?

Oh dear, what can the matter be
With this metal so silvery?
Liquid at 86 degrees,
Gallium melts in my hand.

Germanium: There's a Hole in the Bucket

There's a hole in your table,
Dmitri, Dmitri.
There's a hole in your table,
Between silicon and tin.

Someday you will fill it,
Dear chemist, dear chemist,
You'll find a new element
Like silicon and tin.

But how shall we find it,
Dmitri, Dmitri?
The element that fits between
Silicon and tin?

My table will tell you,
Dear chemist, dear chemist.
It's in the same family as
Silicon and tin.

I see what you're saying,
Dmitri, Dmitri.
Its properties will be like
Silicon and tin.

You've got it, dear chemist,
And further, I tell you.
You'll find that its weight will be
Seventy two.

We found it! Dmitri,
Just like you predicted!
Germanium fits between
Silicon and tin.

Arsenic: Go Tell Aunt Rhody

Go tell Aunt Rhody,
Go tell Aunt Rhody,
Go tell Aunt Rhody,
The old gray goose is dead.

She reached for the goose food,
She reached for the goose food,
But poor nearsighted Rhody
Grabbed arsenic instead.

Selenium: Hey Diddle Diddle

Hey diddle diddle,
I'll ask you a riddle.
What element is named for the moon?
It's in photocells,
And is useful as well,
When you want itchy dandruff cured soon.

Hey diddle diddle,
I'll answer your riddle,
Selenium's named for the moon.
But whatever you do,
Avoid SeH_2
It smells so bad you're likely to swoon.

Bromine: My Bonnie Lies Over the Ocean

Some bromine lies under the ocean,
And bromine is in the Dead Sea,
You'll find bromine inside of seaweed,
But don't bring that bromine to me.

Bromine, bromine,
This red liquid's toxic to me, to me.
Volatile, smells vile,
So don't bring that bromine to me.

Krypton: Star light, Star bright

Star light, star bright,
Can't compete with laser light.
Krypton gas, mixed just right
Makes lasers glow with UV light.

Rubidium: Tom Tom the Piper's Son

Tom, Tom, the piper's son,
Stole a piece of rubidium.
He had to try
To keep it dry,
Cause rubidium's an alkali.

Tom, Tom the piper's son,
Liked to play with rubidium.
He did forget,
And got it wet,
And Tom went flying like a jet.

Strontium: Fee Fi Fo Fum

Fee Fi Fo Fum
I am an isotope of strontium.
Weight of 90 a.m.u
Formed when uranium splits in two.

Fee Fi Fo Fum
I'm radioactive strontium.
When I'm near, run away quick,
Or I'll get in your bones and make you sick.

Yttrium: Over in the Meadow

Over in the d block
Just below Scandium,
Is another rare earth metal,
With the name Yttrium.
Discovered up in Sweden,
Just like Scandium,
Named for Ytterby, the town
Where the ore first came from.

Zirconium: Hush Little Baby

Hush little baby, don't say a word.
Mama's gonna buy you a mockingbird.
And if that mockingbird don't sing,
Mama's gonna buy you a diamond ring.

But diamond rings cost quite a lot,
So much more money than what I've got.
But don't be worried, don't be glum,
I'll buy you a new ring of zirconium.

Niobium: The Old Grey Mare

Forty-one ain't called what it used to be.
Ain't called what it used to be.
Ain't called what it used to be.
Back when Hatchett made his discovery,
He called it columbium.

He called it columbium,
Transition metal 41.
In 1801 he found a new element,
And called it columbium.

Fifty years later, Rose found the same element,
Found the same element,
Found the same element,
And he gave a new name to this element,
And called it niobium.

He called it niobium,
Transition metal 41.
Now 41 ain't called what it used to be,
The table says niobium.

Molybdenum: The Farmer in the Dell

The farmer in the dell,
The farmer in the dell,
Needs some molybdenum
To make his crops grow well.

The farmer plants some seeds,
And clears away the weeds,
Water, sun, but he's not done,
There's something else he needs.

An enzyme he will need.
Nitrogenase is key.
But without molybdenum,
It won't work properly.

For in nitrogenase
There is a special space,
Where an atom of molybdenum
Proudly takes its place.

Technetium: Found a Peanut

Found technetium, Found technetium
Mendeleev gave the key.
It was just where he predicted,
In the space 'neath manganese.

It's unstable, radioactive,
Every isotope decays.
Doctors use one as a tracer,
It's a source of gamma rays.

Hickety, pickety, my black pen,
Great for ladies and gentlemen.
Called the Parker 51,
The tip is made from ruthenium.
A metal hard and tarnish-free,
Part of the platinum family.

Rhodium: White Coral Bells

White golden rings, upon my fingers shine.
Noble metal jewelry is quite sublime.
What makes it glitter white like platinum?
It happens when you plate the gold with rhodium.

Palladium: Tweedledum and Tweedledee

Palladium and platinum
Resolved to have a battle.
When each one said, "There is no doubt,
I am the nobler metal."

Said platinum, "My surface has
A silver, lustrous shine."
Palladium said, "That is nice,
But frankly, so does mine."

"I never rust," said platinum,
"A fact you can't deny."
Palladium said, "That is true,
But frankly, nor do I."

Said platinum, "I'm valuable,
And in very short supply."
Palladium said, "That is nice,
But frankly, so am I."

"To catalyze reactions,
We know platinum is best."
"But I too," replied palladium,
"Am a super catalyst."

"Palladium," said platinum,
"Neither one of us can win.
We both are noble, and furthermore,
I think that we are twins."

Silver: Mirror, Mirror on the Wall

"Mirror, mirror on the wall,
What reflects light best of all?"

"For the perfect looking glass,
Don't use copper, gold or brass.
But silver metal polished bright,
Will reflect each ray of light."

"Mirror, mirror, flat and round,
Where is this wondrous metal found?"

"Jewelry stores are sure to stock it.
And you have some in your pocket.
You've had some silver all this time
It's in your quarters and your dimes."

Cadmium: For He's a Jolly Good Fellow

For he's an artistic fellow,
He wants his paintings to sell, so
He uses cadmium yellow,
The best pigment money can buy.

The best pigment money can buy.
The best pigment money can buy.

He uses cadmium yellow,
Made from cadmium sulfide.

Indium: Blue Bird, Blue Bird

Blue line, blue line in the spectrum,
New line, new line in the spectrum,
Indigo blue in the spectrum,
Where did this color come from?

It's an element, a metal in group thirteen,
Soft and ductile, a metal with a high sheen.
Works your iPad by lighting up the touch screen,
Indium, we shall name it.

Tin: I'm A Little Hunk of Tin

I'm a little hunk of tin.
So many things that I might have been.
Plates and roofs and cooking pans,
But mostly I'm in old tin cans.

Green peas, chicken soup, baked beans and Spam,
All packaged for you inside tin cans. (repeat)

Mixed with copper, I make bronze,
Used in ancient Babylon.
Tools of bronze were once the rage,
Way back in the old Bronze Age.

To be cast as sword was once my plan,
But somehow I ended up an old tin can.

Antimony: Crocodile Song

She sailed away on a bright and sunny day,
In a boat floating down the Nile.
An Egyptian queen, her eye makeup was pristine,
Lines of black in dramatic style.
"My secret, you know, is a substance we call kohl,
Made from antimony sulfide.
This makeup isn't new, Cleopatra used it too,
To keep Marc Antony by her side."

Tellurium: Georgie Porgy

Georgie Porgy pudding and pie,
Kissed the girls and made them cry.
They said, "Your garlic breath ain't fun.
Why did you eat tellurium?"

Iodine: I Never Saw a Purple Cow

I never saw a purple gas,
Till I found some iodine,
And sealed it in a tiny flask,
Then watched while it sublimed.

I never knew that iodide
Could have so many uses.
It makes a super germicide,
To heal your cuts and bruises.

Xenon: Little Jack Horner

Little Jack Horner
Sat in a corner.
With some xenon gas in a tube.
"They say it's a fact
This gas won't react.
But I wonder if that's really true."

To this noble gas xenon,
Little Jack piped in
Some platinum hexafluoride.
To his satisfaction,
He saw a reaction.
"Xenon's not an inert gas," he cried.

Cesium: Hickory, dickory, dock

Hickory, dickory, dock,
Let's build an atomic clock.
To make it run,
Use cesium,
Hickory, dickory, dock.

Barium: Jack Sprat

Jack Sprat ate too much fat,
He gorged on too much cake.
Then one day poor Jack woke up with
A mighty stomach ache.

"Jack Sprat," the doctor said,
"You're sick and that's a fact.
I need to take an X-ray of
Your whole digestive tract."

"No Doc, I think you're wrong,"
Jack Sprat said with a moan,
"I know X-rays are only good
For pictures of a bone."

"Not if you drink barium.
The taste is awful, but,
With barium, my X-rays get
A picture of your gut."

Lanthanum: Jingle Bells

Dashing through the roads
In my Prius hybrid car,
Tank is almost dry,
But I can still go far.

Don't need gasoline,
To make this engine hum.
Instead I have a battery
That's made with lanthanum.

Oh, lanthanum, lanthanum,
Great in batteries.
This rare earth metal lends its name
To the lanthanide series.

Cerium: Jack Be Nimble, Jack Be Quick

Jack be nimble, Jack be quick,
Jack jumped over the candlestick.

How did young Jack light the wick
Of this glowing candlestick?

Jack said "I can get it done
With a flint made with cerium.

Strike the flint and sparks fly off it,
Because cerium is pyrophoric.

That means it has the property
Of igniting spontaneously.

So to light a candlestick,
Get some cerium, double quick."

Neodymium and Praseodymium: Michael Finnegan

I know a metal named praseodymium,
A rare earth lanthanide just like cerium.
It has a twin called neodymium.
Combined they make didymium:
Begin again..

I know a metal named neodymium,
A rare earth lanthanide just like cerium.
It has a twin called praseodymium.
Combined they make didymium:
Begin again..

Promethium: This Old Man

Lanthanide sixty one,
We call it promethium.
It was made in a lab in Oak Ridge Tennessee,
It's known for its radioactivity.

Samarium: Aiken Drum

There is a metal on the moon,
On the moon, on the moon.
There is a metal on the moon,
And it's called samarium.

Chorus:
And it has a real long half-life,
Long half-life, long half-life.
And it has a real long half-life
Of one hundred billion years.

This isotope of samarium,
Samarium, samarium,
Decays to form an isotope
Of neodymium.

Chorus:
And it has a real long half-life
Long half-life, long half-life.
And it has a real long half-life
Of one hundred billion years.

So if you take rocks from the moon,
From the moon, from the moon.
And measure the samarium,
You'll learn the moon's true age.

Europium: Taffy was a Welshman

Taffy was a forger,
Taffy was a thief.
Taffy forged some Euro notes,
And thought they would deceive.

Taffy made a big mistake,
Something really dumb.
Taffy made his Euro notes
Without Europium.

A banker checked his Euro notes,
And said "Something's not right.
A real Euro should glow red
Under a U-V light."

Europium makes Euros glow.
Without it the test fails.
The banker called them forgeries.
And Taffy went to jail.

Gadolinium: I Know an Old Lady Who Swallowed a Fly

I know an old lady who swallowed a fly.
I don't know why
She swallowed the fly.
Perhaps she'll die.

That old lady went to a doctor nearby,
And asked him to try
To get rid of the fly.
So she wouldn't die.

"Old lady," the doctor replied with a sigh,
"To find this fly
I have to rely
On an MRI."

"But first you must swallow a special dye,
That is made with some
Gadolinium.
The dye will allow the MRI
To find the fly
That is hiding inside.
So you won't die."

Up in Ytterby, that's in Scotland,
Excavated from a mine,
Was a black rock, and this black rock
Held a most amazing find.

Chemists named this new ore yttria,
And when it was purified,
They isolated four new elements,
Three of them were lanthanides.

One was terbium, two was erbium,
And ytterbium made three.
Each of these names will recall the fame
Of this mine in Ytterby.

Holmium: Sticks and Stones

Sticks and stones may break my bones,
But names will never hurt me.

Kidney stones cause pain and moans,
And boy, they sure do hurt me.

With holmium, the pain is gone.
They use it in a laser.

It's also great for large prostates.
It cures without incisions.

Hafnium: Hot Cross Buns

Hafnium,
Hafnium,
Hard to separate it from
Zirconium.

Hafnium,
Hafnium,
In nuclear reactors it will
Catch neutrons.
Hafnium,
Hafnium.

Tantalum: Frere Jacques (Brother John)

Are you calling?
Are you calling?
Brother John,
Brother John?
My cell phone is buzzing,
Making noise because in-
Side is some
Tantalum.

In my iphone
In my iphone,
There is some
Tantalum.
Wonder what they use it for?
Charging a capacitor.
Tantalum.
Tantalum.

Tungsten: This Little Light Of Mine

This little light of mine, wonder what makes it shine?
This little light of mine, wonder what makes it shine?
This little light of mine, wonder what makes it shine?
When I plug this bulb into my lamp.

In this light of mine, I see a glowing wire.
A filament so hot, it looks like it's on fire.
Three thousand centigrade won't melt away this wire.
Tungsten wire in my light makes it shine.

Rhenium: The Wheels on the Bus

The turbines on the jet go round and round,
Round and round,
Round and round.
The turbines on the jet go round and round,
To lift it off the ground.

The blades on the turbine get hot, hot, hot,
Hot, hot, hot,
Hot, hot, hot.
But will they ever melt? They'll not, not, not.
Cause they're made with rhenium.

Osmium: Sixteen Tons

You haul sixteen tons, and what do you get?
A truckload of an element—the densest one yet.
It's a shiny metal that won't corrode.
This osmium makes a heavy load.

Iridium: Where Have All the Flowers Gone?

Where have all the dinosaurs gone?
Long time passing.
Where have all the dinosaurs gone?
Long time ago.
Where have all the dinosaurs gone?
Killed by an asteroid, every one.
It crashed to earth with a mighty blow,
Millions of years ago.

How do we know this theory's true?
Long time passing.
Iridium provides the clue.
Long time ago.
Where the asteroid crashed down,
They dug up iridium.
An element more often found
In asteroids than in the ground.

Platinum: Lincoln, Lincoln I've Been Thinking

Lincoln, Lincoln, I've been thinking.
What's that new ring on your pinkie?
Looks like silver,
Costs a ton.
Oh my gosh, it's platinum.

Lincoln, Lincoln drives a green car.
What's the secret to a clean car?
A converter
Makes it hum,
Catalyzed by platinum.

Gold: Old King Cole

Old King Gold was a merry old soul,
And a merry old soul was he.
He shone like the sun,
And he told everyone
"I'm the noblest of metals, you'll agree."

Old King Gold was a shiny old soul,
And he bragged of his luster with glee.
"I tell you no lies.
I do not oxidize.
And you'll never find tarnish on me."

Old King Gold was a heavy old soul,
Yes, a heavy two tons was he.
He said with a groan,
"I can't move off this throne.
Because I weigh 19 grams per c.c."

Mercury: Row, Row, Row Your Boat

Flow, flow, flow along,
Like a silver stream,
Mercury, mercury, mercury, mercury,
See the way it gleams.

Used in thermometers,
And fillings for your teeth.
But do not spill mercury, mercury, mercury.
It's poisonous to breathe.

Thallium: This is the House that Jack Built

This is the house that Jack built.

This is the malt
That lay in the house that Jack built.

This is the rat,
That ate the malt
That lay in the house that Jack built.

This is the poison,
That killed the rat,
That ate the malt
That lay in the house that Jack built.

This is the thallium,
That's in the poison
That killed the rat
That ate the malt
That lay in the house that Jack built.

Lead: There Was a Little Girl Who Had a Little Curl

There was a piece of lead.
And unhappily he said,
"My personality is really quite disordered.
For when I am good, I am very very good.
But when I am bad, I am horrid."

If you ever find you need
A radiation shield,
I'm the element to keep you safe and sound.
My density's so great, I block all the harmful rays.
A better heavy metal can't be found.

But watch out if I taint
Your water or your paint.
You don't want lead in pipes or your faucet.
Have your water tested, because if I'm ingested,
You'll find that I am horribly toxic.

Bismuth: Peas Porridge Hot

Peas porridge hot,
Peas porridge cold,
Peas porridge in the pot,
Nine days old.

I ate it all,
Quite a mistake.
That porridge gave me
A big tummy ache.

Needed relief,
Bismuth did the trick.
It's in Pepto-Bismol,
And cured me quick.

Polonium: Old MacDonald

Madame Curie had some ore.
EIEIO
A ton of pitchblende, maybe more.
EIEIO
With alpha rays here
And alpha rays there,
Here an alpha, there an alpha,
Everywhere were alpha rays.
Madame Curie had some ore.
EIEIO

Said Madame Curie to Pierre,
EIEIO
"There's too much radiation here.
EIEIO
With alpha rays here
And alpha rays there,
I don't know an element
That radiates like this does."
Madame Curie had some ore.
EIEIO

Said Madame Curie to Pierre,
EIEIO
"I think there's a new element here."
EIEIO
With alpha rays here,
And alpha rays there,
They purified, identified
The source of all the alpha rays.
Madame Curie had some ore.
EIEIO

Since Poland's where Marie came from,
EIEIO
They called the new element polonium.
EIEIO
With alpha rays here
And alpha rays there,
Here an alpha, there an alpha,
Everywhere were alpha rays.
Madame Curie had some ore.
EIEIO

Astatine: Oh Where Oh Where has my Little Dog Gone?

Oh where oh where has my astatine gone?
Oh where oh where can it be?
It took less than a day
To decay away.
It lacks all stability.

How rare, how rare is this astatine?
How rare, how rare can it be?
Earth's whole complement
Of this element
Weighs little more than a pea.

Radon: Scotland's Burning

Radon's leaking, Radon's leaking,
In my house, in my house.
No smell, no taste,
Cannot see it,
Still there's danger:
Radiation!

Francium: Shenandoah

Oh Francium
I long to see you
Thrown into a rolling river.
Oh, Francium,
Would we all flee you?
Away, we'd run away
From the loud explosion.

But Fracium,
We'll never see you
Thrown into that rolling river.
Cause Francium,
The rarest alkali,
Decays, decays away.
Because it's radioactive.

Radium: Mary, Mary Quite Contrary

Marie, Marie, Madame Curie,
Why does my watch dial glow?
"The luminescence is from an element
Pierre and I found long ago."

Marie, Marie, Madame Curie,
What can this element be?
"It's radium, and the glow comes from
Its radioactivity."

Uranium: Boom Boom Ain't it Great to be Crazy

Boom boom ain't it great to be uranium?
More powerful than steel or titanium.
Radioactive all day long.
Boom boom ain't it great to be uranium?

Start with uranium 235.
And shoot it with some neutrons to make it divide.
If the chain reaction goes out of control,
The fission energy will make it explode!

Boom boom ain't it great to be uranium?
More powerful than steel or titanium.
Radioactive all day long.
Boom boom ain't it great to be uranium?

If you don't want to build an atomic bomb,
You can keep the reaction slow and calm.
Control rods will slow neutron activity,
So the nuclear power makes electricity.

Periodic Table of the Elements

1 IA 1A																	18 VIIIA 8A
1 H Hydrogen 1.008	2 IIA 2A											13 IIIA 3A	14 IVA 4A	15 VA 5A	16 VIA 6A	17 VIIA 7A	**2 He** Helium 4.003
3 Li Lithium 6.941	**4 Be** Beryllium 9.012											**5 B** Boron 10.811	**6 C** Carbon 12.011	**7 N** Nitrogen 14.007	**8 O** Oxygen 15.999	**9 F** Fluorine 18.998	**10 Ne** Neon 20.180
11 Na Sodium 22.990	**12 Mg** Magnesium 24.305	3 IIIB 3B	4 IVB 4B	5 VB 5B	6 VIB 6B	7 VIIB 7B	8 VIII 8	9 VIII 8	10 VIII 8	11 IB 1B	12 IIB 2B	**13 Al** Aluminum 26.982	**14 Si** Silicon 28.086	**15 P** Phosphorus 30.974	**16 S** Sulfur 32.066	**17 Cl** Chlorine 35.453	**18 Ar** Argon 39.948
19 K Potassium 39.098	**20 Ca** Calcium 40.078	**21 Sc** Scandium 44.956	**22 Ti** Titanium 47.867	**23 V** Vanadium 50.942	**24 Cr** Chromium 51.996	**25 Mn** Manganese 54.938	**26 Fe** Iron 55.845	**27 Co** Cobalt 58.933	**28 Ni** Nickel 58.693	**29 Cu** Copper 63.546	**30 Zn** Zinc 65.38	**31 Ga** Gallium 69.723	**32 Ge** Germanium 72.631	**33 As** Arsenic 74.922	**34 Se** Selenium 78.971	**35 Br** Bromine 79.904	**36 Kr** Krypton 83.798
37 Rb Rubidium 85.468	**38 Sr** Strontium 87.62	**39 Y** Yttrium 88.906	**40 Zr** Zirconium 91.224	**41 Nb** Niobium 92.906	**42 Mo** Molybdenum 95.95	**43 Tc** Technetium 98.907	**44 Ru** Ruthenium 101.07	**45 Rh** Rhodium 102.906	**46 Pd** Palladium 106.42	**47 Ag** Silver 107.868	**48 Cd** Cadmium 112.414	**49 In** Indium 114.818	**50 Sn** Tin 118.711	**51 Sb** Antimony 121.760	**52 Te** Tellurium 127.6	**53 I** Iodine 126.904	**54 Xe** Xenon 131.294
55 Cs Cesium 132.905	**56 Ba** Barium 137.328	57-71	**72 Hf** Hafnium 178.49	**73 Ta** Tantalum 180.948	**74 W** Tungsten 183.84	**75 Re** Rhenium 186.207	**76 Os** Osmium 190.23	**77 Ir** Iridium 192.217	**78 Pt** Platinum 195.085	**79 Au** Gold 196.967	**80 Hg** Mercury 200.592	**81 Tl** Thallium 204.383	**82 Pb** Lead 207.2	**83 Bi** Bismuth 208.980	**84 Po** Polonium [208.982]	**85 At** Astatine 209.987	**86 Rn** Radon 222.018
87 Fr Francium 223.020	**88 Ra** Radium 226.025	89-103	**104 Rf** Rutherfordium [261]	**105 Db** Dubnium [262]	**106 Sg** Seaborgium [266]	**107 Bh** Bohrium [264]	**108 Hs** Hassium [269]	**109 Mt** Meitnerium [278]	**110 Ds** Darmstadtium [281]	**111 Rg** Roentgenium [280]	**112 Cn** Copernicium [285]	**113 Nh** Nihonium [286]	**114 Fl** Flerovium [289]	**115 Mc** Moscovium [289]	**116 Lv** Livermorium [293]	**117 Ts** Tennessine [294]	**118 Og** Oganesson [294]

Lanthanide Series

57 La Lanthanum 138.905	**58 Ce** Cerium 140.116	**59 Pr** Praseodymium 140.908	**60 Nd** Neodymium 144.243	**61 Pm** Promethium 144.913	**62 Sm** Samarium 150.36	**63 Eu** Europium 151.964	**64 Gd** Gadolinium 157.25	**65 Tb** Terbium 158.925	**66 Dy** Dysprosium 162.500	**67 Ho** Holmium 164.930	**68 Er** Erbium 167.259	**69 Tm** Thulium 168.934	**70 Yb** Ytterbium 173.055	**71 Lu** Lutetium 174.967

Actinide Series

89 Ac Actinium 227.028	**90 Th** Thorium 232.038	**91 Pa** Protactinium 231.036	**92 U** Uranium 238.029	**93 Np** Neptunium 237.048	**94 Pu** Plutonium 244.064	**95 Am** Americium 243.061	**96 Cm** Curium 247.070	**97 Bk** Berkelium 247.070	**98 Cf** Californium 251.080	**99 Es** Einsteinium [254]	**100 Fm** Fermium 257.095	**101 Md** Mendelevium 258.1	**102 No** Nobelium 259.101	**103 Lr** Lawrencium [262]